HIROMI'S HANDS

HIROMI'S HANDS

by Lynne Barasch

LEE & LOW BOOKS Inc. • New York

To Dinah and the Suzuki family —*L.B.*

Author's Sources
Imatani, Aya. *Sushi for Wimps: Seaweed to Dragon Rolls for the Faint of Heart.* New
    York: Sterling, 2004.
Japanese Characters. "Kanji."
    www.harapan.co.jp/english/japan/kanji.htm
Louie, Elaine. "She Has a Knife and She Knows How to Use It." *New York Times,*
    June 5, 2002, Dining section.
Sushi-Master. "The History of Sushi."
    www.sushi-master.com/usa/whatis/history.html
Suzuki, Akira. Interviews with Lynne Barasch.
Suzuki, Hiromi. Interviews with Lynne Barasch.
TAKA's California-Style Japanese Cuisine. "The History of Sushi."
    www.takassushi.net/page/page/2040176.htm
Winjutsu.com. "Pronouncing Japanese Words."
    www.winjutsu.com/ninjakids/nk_vocabulary.html

The representations of Japanese writing in the book are for illustrative purposes only and should not
be considered as actual words to be read. Any words that may appear were created by coincidence.

Copyright © 2007 by Lynne Barasch

All rights reserved. No part of the contents of this
book may be reproduced by any means without the
written permission of the publisher.
LEE & LOW BOOKS Inc., 95 Madison Avenue,
New York, NY 10016
leeandlow.com

Manufactured in China

Book design by Tania Garcia
Book production by The Kids at Our House

The text is set in Fournier
The illustrations are rendered in ink and watercolor
10 9 8 7 6 5 4 3 2 1
First Edition

Library of Congress Cataloging-in-Publication Data
Barasch, Lynne.
    Hiromi's hands / by Lynne Barasch. — 1st ed.
        p. cm.
    "A biography of Hiromi Suzuki, a Japanese
American girl who, with her father's guidance, defies
tradition and trains to become a sushi chef at her
family's restaurant in New York City"—Provided by
publisher.
ISBN-13: 978-1-58430-275-9
1. Suzuki, Hiromi—Juvenile literature. 2. Women
cooks—United States—Biography—Juvenile
literature. 3. Sushi—Juvenile literature. I. Title.
TX649.S89B37 2006
641.5092—dc22
[B]   2006017283

The day my parents, Akira and Kaoru Suzuki, left for Japan in 1999 was one they would never forget. They were taking their first vacation in thirty-five years. Mama and Papa were going to visit family they hadn't seen in a long, long time.

Back in Japan, my father grew up in a rural village near Tokyo.
He had seven brothers and sisters, and money was scarce.

In his school photograph, Papa was the only boy without a uniform. His family couldn't afford one.

Papa always accompanied his mother to the fishmonger. He was fascinated by the mounds of fish. His mother remembered this when Papa turned fifteen and had to leave their village to find work.

"Akira, you could be an apprentice to a sushi chef—a fine craft," his mother said. "You'll always make a living, and the fish will remind you of home."

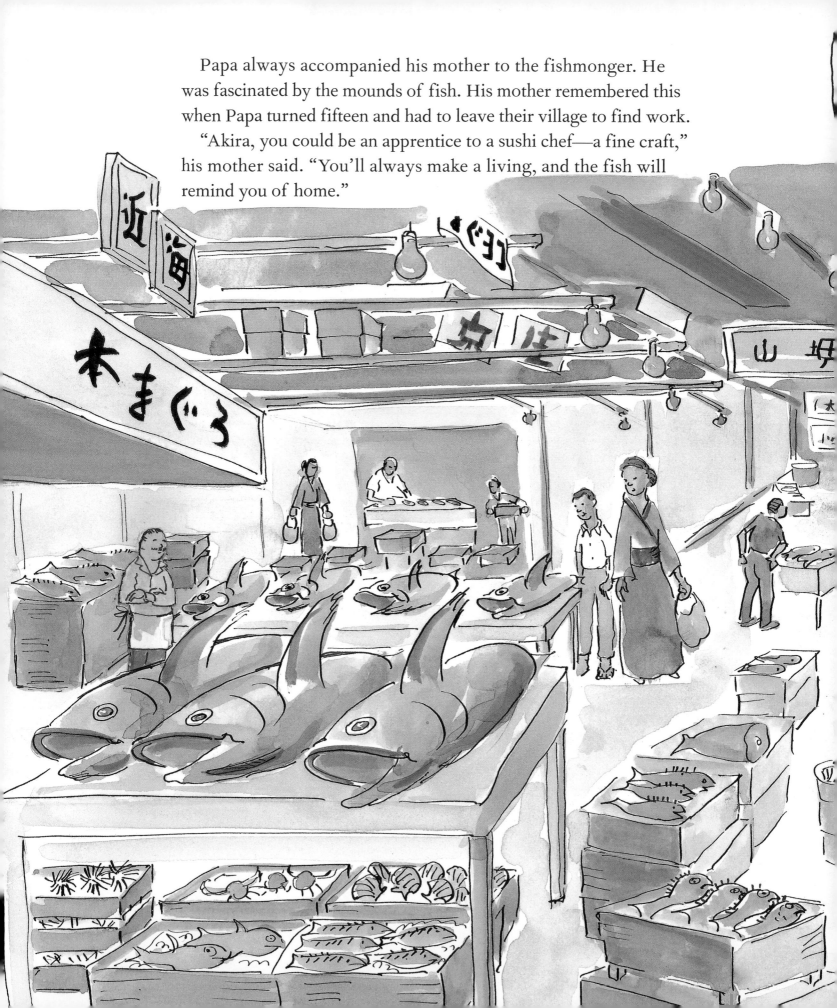

So Papa signed on as an apprentice in the Kamehachi restaurant in Tokyo.

Papa's mother was glad he was a boy. A girl could never be a sushi chef. People thought a woman's soft, warm hands would spoil the fish. Besides, tradition dictated that a woman's place was at home. She ate after her husband finished his meals, and when they went out, she walked behind him.

The first year Papa scrubbed
the kitchen.

He watched the sushi chefs, *itamae*,
make their perfect sushi rolls.

The second year Papa cooked the
rice. On New Year's Day he made
twenty-five batches of rice!

By the third year Papa began to cut fish
with a very sharp knife called a *yanagi*.
After seven more years of learning to
make sushi, he became a full-fledged chef.
He worked twelve hours every day, with
only one day off each month.

Ten years later, in 1964, Papa received exciting news. Kamehachi's
New York restaurant needed a chef. They had chosen him!

New York amazed Papa. He could get a drink by putting a coin in the slot of a machine. Women were everywhere—in the streets, on subways, in the shops, working in offices. It was "ladies first" in elevators and through doorways. There were big cars, big portions, big opportunities!

"Yutaka!" Papa exclaimed. New York was abundant, plentiful
in so many ways. He loved it all.

Papa worked at Kamehachi fifteen hours a day. He lived simply and saved most of his salary. After three years he could afford to open his own restaurant. He called it Akasaka.

One day friends came into Papa's restaurant with a young woman named Kaoru. They were introduced. Was it the fish? Was it the rice? We will never know, but Papa and Mama fell in love that day.

A year later, in 1978, my mother presented Papa with a tiny package—me! Papa thought I was more precious than the most perfect sushi. They named me Hiromi.

Soon they were married.

I grew quickly into a sturdy, happy little girl.

All week I went to school with my friends. Then on Saturday
I went to Japanese school. I learned to read and write Japanese. I
learned about Japanese traditions.

Every year in early February we celebrated Setsuban, the day
before the first day of spring. We cleaned our apartment. Then
we scattered beans to chase away evil and welcome in happiness.

On March third we observed Hinamatsuri, Girls' Day. This is a day when people pray for young girls to be healthy and happy. We displayed dolls and peach blossoms. The dolls were handed down from my grandmother to Mama to me.

I respected the old customs and traditions of Japan, but I also wanted to be like my friends. We were in America. Japan was far away.

I didn't see much of Papa. His day began early in the morning and went straight through until ten at night. The only time we had together was Sundays, when the restaurant was closed.

I missed Papa. I wished I could spend more time with him.

When I was eight years old, I went to see Papa after school one day. "May I go to the fish market with you?" I asked.

Papa was surprised. "Hiromi, the Fulton Fish Market is no place for a child," he said.

I wouldn't take no for an answer. I pleaded until Papa gave in.

We left for the fish market before the sun came up. The market
was loud and smelly.

"No talking," Papa said. "This is serious business."

I kept close to him, but I had many questions.

"What fish is this?" I asked, soon forgetting Papa's warning.
"What's that?" I wanted to know about every fish in the market.
At first Papa didn't answer. Then he realized I was really
interested. He began to teach me.

On a typical day Papa bought tuna, salmon, bonito, mackerel, various clams, and fluke. I laughed when he showed me how fluke was different from the other fish. Fluke has both eyes on the same side of its head!

We loaded all the fish into a shopping cart and then put
it in the back of our old beat-up car. Papa drove me home
so I could go to school. He went on to the restaurant to get
the fish ready for making sushi.

I went to the Fulton Fish Market many times with Papa. I learned more and more.

When Papa touched a fish I did the same.

"Your fingers should not leave a dent," Papa explained. "Firm is fresh. Soft is not. Notice the eyes too. They should be clear. The fins should not be broken."

I loved the time I spent with Papa at the fish market. I loved being part of his grown-up world.

When I was thirteen, once again I went to Papa.

"May I help you at the restaurant?" I asked. I took pride in my knowledge of all of the fish. I wanted to learn to make sushi like my father. I wanted to become a sushi chef.

Papa could see how excited I was.

"If you really want to do this, I will let you try," he said. "You know fish as well as any man. And this is America. Girls can do things here that they cannot do in Japan. Who knows? You might even become *itamae-san*!"

And so I began my apprenticeship, helping
Papa after school and on weekends.

I scrubbed the kitchen floor.

I learned to make the rice. I washed
the grains, then steamed the rice.

I tossed the cooked rice with seasonings
and fanned it so it would cool quickly.
This gave the rice a glossy appearance.

Papa was demanding and the work was hard. I knew his high standards were meant to teach me to be the best chef I could be.

It took three years until I got my own *yanagi* and began cutting fish.

Eventually I mastered every type of sushi. I could shape the rice into ovals and lay small slices of fish over them. I could wrap the rice and fish tightly in *nori*, the seaweed used to make sushi rolls. Finally I could turn out beautiful sushi, just like Papa's.

NIGIRI SUSHI
(SEAFOOD OVER PRESSED RICE)

Kurodai (sea bream)   Shima-aji (yellowjack)   Sake (salmon)   Maguro (tuna)   Ebi (shrimp)

MAKI SUSHI
(RICE AND OTHER INGREDIENTS ROLLED TOGETHER)

GUNKANMAKI (BATTLESHIP OR BOAT ROLL)

Ikura (salmon roe)

Maguro uzura (tuna and quail egg)

Negi shima-aji (scallion and yellowjack)

HOSOMAKI (THIN ROLL)

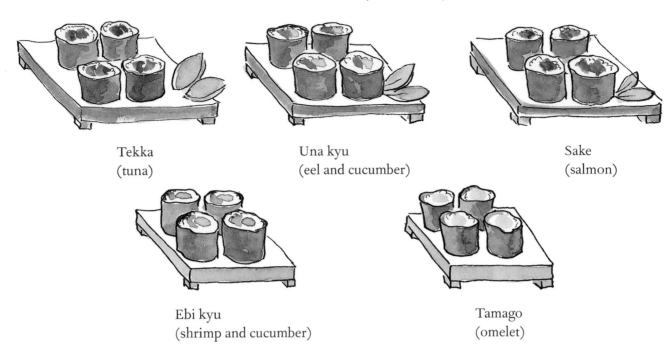

Tekka
(tuna)

Una kyu
(eel and cucumber)

Sake
(salmon)

Ebi kyu
(shrimp and cucumber)

Tamago
(omelet)

URAMAKI (INSIDE-OUT ROLL)

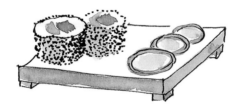

Maguro taku
(tuna and pickled radish)

California roll
(imitation crab, avocado,
and cucumber)

FUTOMAKI (THICK OR LARGE ROLL)

Ebi unagi
(shrimp and eel)

TEMAKI (HAND ROLL)

Negi maguro
(scallion and tuna)

I was ready to begin work as a sushi chef with my father at Akasaka.

One day in 1998 we had a surprise. Mr. Ito, the owner of Kamehachi restaurant in Tokyo, came in for lunch. He greeted my father warmly, but he was shocked to see me behind the counter.

"I trained Hiromi myself," said Papa. "Let her show you what she can do."

Nervously I prepared sushi for Mr. Ito. My fingers flew, wrapping and rolling just so, though my mind was in a whirl. Would I be able to slice the fish perfectly, roll the rice tightly, and present the dish with artistry, as I had been taught?

Mr. Ito watched me silently. Then it was his turn to
be surprised.

He popped one piece of sushi into his mouth. Then another.
And another. He ate every piece.

"That was as good as the sushi at Kamehachi in Tokyo!" Mr. Ito
said. "Congratulations. You are truly *itamae-san*."

I was so proud! That was the first time anyone had said those
words to me.

They were just the words Papa needed to hear. After so many years working in the restaurant, he finally put down his *yanagi*, and he and Mama went off to Japan.

He knew Akasaka was in good hands—my hands!

Author's Note

I first met Hiromi Suzuki in 1983 as a five-year-old kindergartener in my daughter Dinah's class. They became lifelong friends. It was Dinah who suggested I write about Hiromi and how she became a sushi chef.

Akira Suzuki, Hiromi's father, came to New York in 1964. Although he trained in the all-male sushi chef tradition of his native Japan, Akira adopted new ideas in the United States. He was willing to teach his daughter his craft, and in 1998 Hiromi became one of the first female sushi chefs in New York.

Akira sold his restaurant in 2004 and retired. He does occasional catering jobs and would like to do more traveling. Hiromi attended culinary

Hiromi Suzuki with her yanagi

school and is currently working at a Japanese restaurant in New York City.

In 2005 the Fulton Fish Market moved from downtown Manhattan to the Bronx. Now Akira and Hiromi can visit the fish market in this story only in their memories.

Sushi developed from an ancient Southeast Asian method of preserving food. Fresh fish was salted and packed with rice. As the fish fermented, the rice produced a substance that preserved the fish. The process took a very long time. When the fish was ready to eat, the rice was discarded.

Around the eighth century this method of food preservation was introduced into Japan. The Japanese developed a way to shorten the process. They began to eat the fish while it was partly raw, along with the rice.

In the early 1800s a chef named Yohei Hanaya began to serve fresh raw fish over rice at his food stall in Edo, as Tokyo was then called. This was the beginning of the current style of sushi. After an earthquake in 1923, many chefs left Edo, taking sushi to other cities around Japan. Today sushi is eaten all over the world.

Lynne Barasch, 2006

Glossary and Pronunciation Guide

The following names and words are adapted from Japanese for spoken English. Some variations in pronunciation may exist.

NAMES

Akasaka *(ah-kah-sah-kah)*

Akira *(ah-kee-rah)*

Hinamatsuri *(hin-ah-mah-soo-ree)*: Girls' Day or Doll Festival, when people pray for the happiness and health of young girls; celebrated on March 3

Hiromi *(hee-roh-mee)*

Ito *(ee-toh)*

Kamehachi *(kah-meh-hah-chee)*

Kaoru *(kah-oh-roo)*

Setsuban *(seht-soo-bahn)*: festival celebrating the day before the first day of spring; falls on February 3 or 4, depending on the year

Suzuki *(soo-ʒoo-kee)*

WORDS

itamae-san *(ee-tah-mah-eh-sahn)* / itamae *(ee-tah-mah-eh)*: professional sushi chef(s)

sushi *(soo-shee)*: vinegared rice; any dish that includes this rice

yanagi *(yah-nah-gee)*: sharp knife used for cutting fish

yutaka *(yoo-tah-kah)*: abundant, enriching, plentiful

SUSHI

ebi *(eh-bee)*: shrimp

futomaki *(foo-toh-mah-kee)*: thick or large sushi roll

gunkanmaki *(goon-kahn-mah-kee)*: sushi battleship or boat roll

hosomaki *(hoh-soh-mah-kee)*: thin sushi roll

ikura *(ee-koo-rah)*: salmon roe

kurodai *(koo-roh-die)*: sea bream

kyu *(cue)* / kyuri *(cue-ree)*: cucumber

maguro *(mah-goo-roh)*: tuna

maki *(mah-kee)*: type of sushi in which vinegared rice and other ingredients are rolled together; usually wrapped in nori

negi *(neh-gee)*: scallion

nigiri *(nee-ghee-ree)*: type of sushi in which a small piece of seafood is placed on top of an oval of pressed, vinegared rice

nori *(nor-ee)*: seaweed

sake *(sah-kay)*: salmon

shima-aji *(shee-mah-ah-jee)*: yellowjack

taku *(tah-koo)* / takuan *(tah-koo-ahn)*: pickled radish

tamago *(tah-mah-goh)*: omelet

tekka *(tek-kah)*: tuna

temaki *(teh-mah-kee)*: sushi hand roll

una *(oo-nah)* / unagi *(oo-nah-gee)*: eel

uramaki *(oo-rah-mah-kee)*: inside-out sushi roll

uzura *(oo-ʒoo-rah)*: quail egg